SKY TRUCK

SKY TRUCK

Stephen Piercey

Osprey Colour Series

First published in 1984 by Osprey Publishing Limited
27A Floral Street, London WC2E 9DP
Member company of the George Philip Group
Reprinted winter 1985 and 1986

British Library Cataloguing in Publication Data

Piercey, Stephen
    Sky Truck.—(Osprey
    colour series)
    I. Sky Truck
    i. Title
    629.133′34023′0222   TL685.4

ISBN 0-85045-552-9

Editor Dennis Baldry
Designed by Norman Brownsword
Printed in Hong Kong

Sky Truck is the result of more than ten years travelling to record the dwindling number of spirited operators who still use fleets of old transport aircraft, against all odds. Who wants to fly a Sky Truck? In a world of jet technology the reasons for the continued operation of aircraft which most people believe passed away ages ago may not be clear, but they are many and varied.

Airlines from Third World countries, for example, may have little choice or may not be able to afford to update their tired fleets. In the early 1980s, however, the situation has changed, leaving few that remain in this category. A prime example of an airline making do with outdated equipment is Air Tchad. The troubled nation's only airline relies on a passenger DC-3 and DC-4 to serve its busy network from N'djamena. During 1983 the weary DC-4, flagship of the line, was airlifting the wounded from war-torn northern Chad alongside the air force's only transport, another DC-4 that apparently never flies on more than three engines. A substantial number of propeller-driven transports which have served with front-line airlines, particularly in Europe, have been forced out of service by increasing costs and the relative scarcity of avgas. An example is the departure, in 1982, of Europe's last two commercially operated DC-6s.

Then there are the smaller, more colourful cargo operators, often one-man bands running on less than a shoestring budget. They ply back-street cargo markets, seeking work, and carry literally anything that will pass through their cargo doors.

Finally at the bottom end of the scale, but mass users of old piston-engined equipment, are the 'dopers', hotly pursued by the grossly overworked Drug Enforcement Administration (DEA). Vast amounts of cash are awaiting owners of the piston giants – in any condition – should they be prepared to lose their aircraft in the process. Pilots, too, may be tempted by very substantial cash offers approaching the half a million dollar mark to run a mission down south to collect an illicit cargo from some dirt strip and return with an often overladen aeroplane. But the game is becoming increasingly risky, although the prospect of an extended stay in a Colombian jail does not appear to deter everybody.

Whether these giants of a past era retire with grace, are impounded, abandoned, or scrapped, or whether they are placed in a used-plane lot or terminate their careers in the side of a mountain or in some steamy jungle, their days are numbered. *Sky Truck* is a tribute to the great and often brave characters who struggle to keep their machines in the air.

Although he is unable to recollect transatlantic crossings by DC-7C and Britannia aircraft at the age of two, Stephen Piercey has been devoted to propeller-driven transport aircraft since the early 1960s. His earliest memory is of a Constellation on finals to London Airport. His lifelong interest has taken him across the world. Such is his love for these flying crocks that he has travelled half a million miles since 1973, seeking them out. In pursuit of his unusual hobby Stephen Piercey has made more than 150 flights aboard piston engined aircraft – often in difficult circumstances – and on occasions has been known to share flights, not always willingly, with pigs, cows, bulls, chickens, horses, avocados, mangoes, bananas, and a party of Jehova's Witnesses.

Aged 26, Stephen Piercey works as chief photographer for the British aviation weekly *Flight International*. During 1978 he formed *Propliner* aviation magazine as an extension to his hobby. This quality quarterly review of historic and current propeller transport operations now sells in more than 35 countries.

To 'Bud' McNair, Duncan Baker and Bill Whitesell – great aviators.

Appreciation

On 20 May 1984, shortly before *Sky Truck* was published, Stephen Piercey and his *Flight* colleague Cliff Barnett were killed when their Aztec cameraship was involved in a mid-air collision. Steve was only 27 years of age.

When I joined *Flight International* magazine in 1978, my desk was within ear-shock of an ebullient, outrageous individual who seemed to be a walking sound-effects department thinly disguised as a picture librarian. Steve's impersonations of a quartet of Merlins on final approach, followed by the piercing squeals of rubber on concrete, were a joy—another Argonaut had landed. I entered into the spirit of it, but my rendering of a Gipsy Major Mk 8 running-up was pathetic by comparison.

The passage of time gave me the happy opportunity to commission Steve to produce *Sky Truck*. His superb photography, professionalism, energy, and humour created a very special book. I will miss Steve as a friend and a colleague. *Sky Truck* is his memorial.

Dennis Baldry
Osprey Publishing
London, January 1985

Contents

Pounding pistons

Colombia has always been a haven for old piston-engined aircraft. Conscious of poor safety records, its Government wishes to abolish reciprocating airliners from its skies within five years. Lineas Aereas del Caribe (LAC) of northern Colombia flies an immaculate fleet of Douglas DC-6As, although it has lost a number in fatal accidents. LAC is proud of its newly acquired DC-8 jets, and is phasing-out its DC-6s. Seen taxying from Miami's northwest cargo area with 30,000 lb of industrial machinery, DC-6 HK-1707, in its 51,038th hour, flew into a mountain near Chiquinquira, north of Bogota, while on a flight from Trinidad to the Colombian capital in December 1978

9

Bolivia could not exist without its faithful Curtiss Commandos. Written off with great regularity, these old WW2 work-horses are either rebuilt or are replaced by other C-46s that can be bought at knock-down prices from South or North America. Sole fleet member of Transportes Aereos San Martin (TASMA) flies from La Paz, Bolivia, and was seen departing from its base in 1977, dutifully watched by the company's entire staff. Within 30 minutes she was back on the ramp after suffering a blown engine on take-off – actually the third Bolivian C-46 to lose an engine that morning

About 100 C-46s remain active. They offer a generous payload and the type remains competitive, although poor single-engine performance has caused many a ditching. This natural metal C-46, N1807M, has changed hands many times, but remains based out of Miami's Corrosion Corner

Florida's La Mancha Aire was formed to operate Douglas DC-7 freighters during 1979. Its first aircraft, a DC-7B, was rebuilt from scratch by the airline at a cost of $400,000. Illustrated is its second aircraft (since sold), a former BOAC DC-7C. N16465 fires up her massive Wright 3350s at Port of Spain, Trinidad. Her cargo? 36,000 lb of toilet rolls and biscuits destined for a Caribbean island

Routine 3-engined arrival: Number two engine feathered, this DC-6B of Transportes Aereos Mercantiles Panamericanos (TAMPA) arrives at its Medellin base in central Colombia. Now an all-jet operator, TAMPA has a well-earned reputation in the drug world. It has been caught red-handed more than once with massive drug hauls in the bellies of its Boeing 707s. One such cargo, labelled 'blue jeans', was worth an estimated 20 billion dollars in street value

Passenger-carrying Lockheed Constellations remained operational as late as January 1979. Aerovias Quisqueyana of the Dominican Republic was the final passenger operator anywhere, and offered twice-daily, regularly overbooked services in its 80-seat 049 and 749 aircraft between Santo Domingo and San Juan. Early morning travellers were given a cup of rum instead of coffee. This 1946-vintage 049 was retired in 1977. It is remarkable that she was still taking passenger fares so late in life, and ironic that the last Constellations to carry passengers were the oldest in existence

Cargo Curtiss Commandos and passenger Viscounts comprise the fleet of Aeropesca, a small established Colombian carrier. C-46 HK-388, seen at its Bogota base, went missing on a flight from Medellin to Barranquilla in October 1981. She was later found abandoned floating in the River Orteguaza, south west Colombia. Only 1500 km from its original route, the old Commando had been hijacked by left-wing guerillas who forced the crew to fly to Panama, where crates of arms were loaded

A typically smokey start-up for a Super Constellation's Wright 3350. In later life, overhaul times for these temperamental engines averaged 1200 hr, although some operators were known to pass the 3000 hr mark

OVERLEAF This old Boeing B-17 Flying Fortress was not kept operational in Bolivia as a historic memorial to the last war, but was flown commercially! Operated by Frigorificos Reyes, CP-891 was the last of the cargo B-17s. Flying from La Paz, she earned long overdue retirement in a USAF museum in California

Thundering across Miami International Airport, Cayman Airways' DC-6B N61267 was lease-purchased from Rich International. Operating regular runs from Grand Cayman island, she was later repossessed for non-payment

This mighty Lockheed 1649 Starliner was being
prepared during 1983 for her first flight since 1976.
Her new owner, Maine-born Maurice Roundy, is a
self-confessed Connie buff. During the late summer the
1649's engines were turning for the first time in seven
years

For just a few dollars you too may experience an exhilarating ride through Colombia's Cordillera Mountains in a DC-4 of SATENA, transport wing of the Colombian Air Force. Operating to airstrips and bush clearings that no other carrier would contemplate, SATENA's rugged fleet are manned by proficient military personnel. FAC1105 was photographed at Villavicencio, an hour's flight east of Bogota. She was damaged beyond repair in a landing accident. Sistership FAC1106 RIGHT was destroyed in December 1979 when she flew into high ground while on a flight from Arauca to Cucuta, Colombia, claiming 21 lives. Replacement DC-4s are drafted from the air force inventory as required

OVERLEAF Squatting on a ramp in northern Quebec with thousands of gallons of chemicals in her cabin tanks, this Constellation 749 is ready to begin her day's work at six in the morning spraying spruce budworm. The four to six-week spraying season in Quebec results in millions of acres of forrested land being treated against the villainous budworm

Unusual attitude for a Curtiss Commando landing at Bluefields, Nicaragua, ably demonstrated by AN-BRG. Loaded with 50 passengers, the packed Commando had just completed six sectors from Managua, and was scheduled for two more before the day was out. The airstrips leave a lot to be desired, and several serious accidents have been known to occur. All in a day's work!

LEFT Crying out for mechanical (and cosmetic) attention, a hard-working Douglas DC-4 of Frigorificos Reyes arrives back at its La Paz base on three engines. Offloaded and reloaded within a couple of hours, CP-1207 was airborne again en route to another meat farm in the Bolivian hinterland

OVERLEAF Cold country Canadair: The National Aeronautical Establishment's North Star, CF-SVP-X, seen in the Arctic operating her final mission in April 1976. Her growling Merlins performed well in temperatures of minus 30° or below. Retired and auctioned to a Texan dealer, this last flyable example was later impounded in one of the Bahamas islands

Airborne

Tucking up her wheels out of Edmonton is Douglas DC-4 C-FGNI of Eldorado Aviation, a remarkable private Canadian operator. A division of Eldorado Nuclear, the company has been flying since 1944 and until 1980 used two spotless DC-3s and DC-4s to supply the Uranium City mine in Saskatchewan and other sites in northern Canada with company cargo and personnel. Eldorado disposed of its trusty piston fleet. It now flies a Boeing 737

LEFT Dakota promota: Air Atlantique is Britain's last commercial DC-3 operator, and its flexible fleet of cargo and passenger aircraft are frequent sights at many European airports, or beyond. Illustrated is G-AMPO, operating a flight over Welsh countryside. Retaining the colours of previous owner Eastern Airways, the Dak has now been repainted in Atlantique's dramatic livery

Aptly titled DC-3s and Convair 440s served points in the sunshine state of Florida with Air Sunshine during the 1970s. Absorbed by Air Florida in 1979, Air Sunshine offered bargain $50 day trips to Disneyworld from Miami by one of its friendly 36-seat Daks – satisfaction guaranteed

Television star: Owned and operated by the Aces High film facilities group, this Douglas C-47 Dakota was rescued from a military fire dump, and has since become known throughout the world as the star in the television series 'Airline'. Masquerading as 'G-AGHY' of Ruskin Air Services, Dakota G-DAKS was photographed performing over her Duxford, Cambridge base

There is good reason for this Super Constellation to fly
with her overwing emergency exits removed. It was an
attempt to reduce the intense heat in the cabin given
off by terrified livestock. On the Connie's empty return
sectors it was an attempt to reduce the aroma of a six-
inch layer of dung deposited on the cabin floor by the
outward-bound cargo! The aircraft, N1007C, was seen
on finals to Miami in September 1977

This remarkable executive-configured DC-3 has served Goodyear in Canada for 35 continuous years. Hangared all her life, she flies up to 14 board members out of Toronto

OVERLEAF Loaded with 7000 lb of chopped cattle, this old Flying Fortress barely cleared the tops of the Bolivian Cordillera's near Choquecamata on her return from Santiago with a freshly slaughtered catch in 1977. At an altitude of 17,500 ft over the mountains her crew and one passenger took turns to make use of an oxygen bottle and air pipe

The number of active DC-7s is rapidly dwindling. Photographed from the right hand seat of a DC-7 camership in close formation is La Mancha Aire's N16465, performing near the Venezuelan coast in 1982. The previous evening she had flown horses down to Rochambeau, French Giuana

Beautiful old Constellation N6021C flew from Miami
for many years with Mack McKendree's Unlimited
Leasing, Inc. Sold in 1979, the 749 was seized in
northern Florida with a 36,000 lb cargo of marijuana.
After five years in open storage the Connie was flown
away by a brave Dominican aircrew in August 1983 for
a new life in the Caribbean

LEFT Many 'reciprocating' aircrew are proud to be
flying the last of the piston giants – others are not so
prop-proud. The fools long for the day they can climb
into a jet

Constellation 749 N6021C nears the Miami Beach area on long finals to Miami. Barely months after this shot was taken the old Connie was on finals to some dirt strip in northern Colombia to collect a multi-million dollar cargo of marijuana. She was one that did not get away, being seized in Panama City, Florida

OVERLEAF The dawn silence of a peaceful town in Quebec is shattered as Conifair Aviation's Constellation C-GXKO claws skywards for an early morning spraying sortie in June 1981

Ideal spraying time for the 'budworm bombers' is
when the air is stillest, early morning or evening.
Captured from an Aztec chase plane, one of the
Connies is seen in action one evening in the region of
Matane, Quebec. Its chemical 'cargo' is coloured to aid
visual monitoring

The last Bristol Freighters flying outside New Zealand are two with Instone Air Line. ZK-EPD, sporting an all-white livery after overhaul, formated alongside the airline's first Bristol 170, G-BISU, on her arrival in British airspace after an agonizingly slow 85 hr delivery flight from Auckland through eight countries. The two Stansted-based Freighters are clocking up hours on ad hoc charters, and are frequently called out at short notice to transport spare engines to stranded wide-bodied jets

The last mission for the National Research Council's Canadair North Star was a week-long aerial survey trip across the Canadian Arctic under the callsign 'Research 8'. A magnetometer was housed in a 25 ft tail boom, visible TOP in a view of the aeroplane taking off from Resolute Bay, North West Territories. Such was the stillness, the North Star was still audible 15 min later. Steep rock formations on Devon Island form a backdrop to the singing Merlins, during a 1000 ft survey near Powell Inlet. When the North Star returned to her Ottawa base at the end of the week she had only 10 engine hours remaining

The majority of active DC-6s may be found in North, South and Central America. While the type has probably carried its last fare-paying passenger, it will remain in service for many more years. Under Colombian ownership this DC-6 was seized in Kansas during 1977 after landing on a highway in the middle of the night with a large consignment of marijuana. Today she is Miami based as N6584C

OVERLEAF Just six Britannias remain active in late 1983, five of which fly out of Zaire in Central Africa. Redcoat Air Cargo was one of Britain's last operators of the type, and its ill-fated G-BRAC was photographed over Swindon on approach to Lyneham one summer's evening in 1978

Turnround

A 10,000 mile ferry flight across the African and South American continents was completed by this 26-year old DC-7C in 1982, after she was bought by La Mancha Aire of Florida from Affretair, Zimbabwe. She was seen at Recife, Brazil, where fuel was uplifted

LEFT Classic lines of the big 'Dougs' are so evident in this full frontal of Rich International's N61267. She awaited her crew for a flight to the Cayman Islands, but the lack of a Cuban overfly permit resulted in a delayed departure

During the long ferry flight from Harare, Zimbabwe, to Florida via the Ivory Coast (West Africa), Brazil, Surinam and Venezuela, La Mancha Aire paid more in fuel costs than it did for the aeroplane. Still retaining Affretair colours, VP-YTY basked in Abidjan sunshine, ready to cross the South Atlantic Ocean to Brazil on the second leg of the trip

A timeless view across the Frigorificos Reyes freight ramp at La Paz. The B-17 (from which the photo was taken) had just returned from a meat farm in the province of Beni, while the DC-4 was preparing to leave on its round to San Borja and Santa Ana, Bolivia. The long-disused control tower, in the background, was full of old and dust-layered radio equipment

OVERLEAF Frigorificos Reyes DC-4 CP-1207 is one of five owned, but rarely are they all in service at one time. Under the supervision of a stray dog, like so many wild animals a habitant of La Paz Airport, the aircraft awaits a cargo for some unheard of – certainly isolated – Bolivian destination

During 1978 more than 30 DC-6s were flying out of Willow Run Airport, Detroit, in support of the three giant US car manufacturers – Ford, General Motors and Chrysler. The recession affected this industry badly, leaving large fleets without work. Trans Continental Airlines survived, but its once large fleet has been reduced to a couple of aircraft

Island trader: One of many Dakotas that ply their trade
around the Caribbean islands is the San Juan-based,
wheel-spatted N80617. Flying with St Maarten
Traders, she hauled a cargo of fish to Tortola in the
British Virgin Islands during March 1980

An everyday scene at Bogota's *El Dorado* Airport. An Aerovias Colombianas DC-3 receives mechanical attention in the open, and a fresh coat of paint

Early model 1049 HI-228 is the oldest flying Super Constellation. Based at Santo Domingo for many years with Aerotours Dominicano, she now flies with Aerochago SA of the same city under a lease agreement with Aerotours. Photographed uplifting produce in St Croix, HI-228 remains as the last commercially operated Connie anywhere – for the time being

La Mancha Aire's DC-7C N16465 loads late in the afternoon in preparation for an early morning departure down to the islands. LMA has been hit by the cargo trade recession. A year ago it flew three DC-7s – today only one remains in service

LMA's DC-7 arrives in the picturesque island of St Kitts, and a 1931 Austin that has definitely seen better days offloads boxes of biscuits and cheese balls, the latter a Christmas delicacy on the island!

This 049 Connie was one of the oldest surviving in the 1970s. She always flew chock-a-block with Quisqueyana on the Santo Domingo–San Juan route, in direct competition with Dominicana de Aviacion (727) and Eastern Airlines (L-1011). Eventually the Dominican Republic Government pulled the carrier's licence in January 1979 on the grounds that its fleet of two serviceable Constellations was unsafe

LEFT For many years two COPA Dakotas linked Bocas del Toro, Changuinola and David with Panama City

OVERLEAF A few years ago LACSA of Costa Rica still flew two pristine C-46s on domestic passenger services. TI-LRB *Chorotega* was seen at the lovely coastal town of Golfito. The runway here is a public road, closed to traffic when aircraft are heard approaching

Beefy Boeing: Flying Fortress meat wagon CP-891 taxies in to her base at La Paz, stirring up clouds of dust in the process. Two of her crew served on B-17s in the last war, and who could have believed that they would still be flying the aeroplane nearly 40 years later?

RIGHT Bolivian mechanics show more interest in the foreigner than their work. A few problems were rectified on No 4 engine before a late morning flight

BOTTOM At a distant meat farm in Santiago, 100 miles east of San Jose de Chiquitos, in eastern Bolivia, the B-17 is loaded with slaughtered cattle destined for markets in La Paz. One may be misled into believing that Frigorificos Reyes has refrigeration units in its aircraft (or at its base). Readers may be assured that there were no such facilities

Laden with general cargo for Trinidad, Bolivia, the
Flying Fortress departs for the second time in a busy
day

A local Bolivian girl at La Paz in company with a flock of sheep and a Flying Fortress

OVERLEAF Spray bars with 68 nozzles each side are attached to the wing trailing edge of this Conifair Constellation. Inside the fuselage are two large tanks which hold about 3000 gallons of 'goop', a term used for the oil and chemical mixture with which they spray

TOP LEFT Former USAF Constellation 749 entered
service with Aerolineas Argo of the Dominican
Republic as HI-328 in 1979 following 10 years as a
Wyoming-based sprayer. She island hopped in the
Caribbean with fresh produce until one starlit night in
October 1981 when her crew flew her into the sea off
the coast of St Thomas. Argo replaced the wrecked
Connie with a sistership, but this, too, was grounded
after the company ceased trading early in 1983

LEFT Another DC-7B that eagerly awaits the summer
season of forest fires is T & G Aviation's 'borate
bomber' N51701. Note the large tank slung underneath
her belly. The cabin of the aircraft is empty

Large numbers of surplus military Douglas C-54s have
found a ready market in the US as sprayers or borate
bombers. Biegert Aviation's fleet of Arizona-based
sprayers were seen from a low flying Cessna, patiently
awaiting the start of a new season

This one-time Delta Air Lines flagship was 26 years old in November 1983. DC-7B N4887C flies on contract aerial firefighting missions from bases in the western USA. She was seen in Arizona being spruced up before a US Forestry Service inspection so that she could take part in the demanding 1981 fire season

Conifair started fighting the budworm in 1979 with a fleet of three Constellations. The spotless, ever-growing fleet today consists of two Connies, four DC-4s and three DC-6s

OVERLEAF The future of these chicks being offloaded from a DC-6 at Borinquen was bleak. Destined to be consumed by Puerto Ricans within days, they had been flown in thousands down from Miami by a pressurised DC-6A belonging to Trans-Air-Link. In the foreground, the one that got away? Unfortunately not. There was no escape from a hungry Puerto Rican on this occasion

With a somewhat suspicious overall-olive green paint scheme, this anonymous DC-6 had been impounded at Santo Domingo early in 1980, although airport officials would not comment on the reason for her being laid up on the far side of the airfield. Similar liveries on other aircraft have proved to be advantageous while flying to small strips in South America

LEFT The political situation in Nicaragua did little to help the ailing flag carrier LANICA during its final years. Its fleet of four cargo DC-6Bs was sold, three of which were caught with cargoes of drugs. On three engines, one DC-6 failed to complete an overshoot at an airfield in West Virginia during June 1979. It crashed in flames on the Kanawha County Airport, burning a ten-ton cargo of marijuana. Earlier, the same aeroplane had run-off a runway in Florida while making a night take-off with an illicit cargo. AN-BFO, pictured while serving with LANICA at its Managua base in 1977, was later seized at Antigua after operating an illegal flight

Finnish carrier Kar-Air's spotless swing-tail DC-6B OH-KDA was one of two aircraft so converted by SABENA at Brussels in 1968. She operated the Helsinki-London cargo schedule for Finnair in the early 1980s, until replaced by a DC-9. Photographed at Manchester shortly before operating one of the last trips from England, OH-KDA was sold during 1982 and now flies for a respectable operator in Florida

RIGHT Want a Britannia? AFREK's two Britannia 253Cs plied the airlanes for many years between Athens and Nigeria with private cargo and personnel for a Greek construction company. Closing its operation in 1983, the Britannias remain stored at Athens and are up for grabs at £200,000 apiece. They were the last civil Britannias to fly in Europe

OVERLEAF Channel Islands-based Lanzair's Super Constellation N11SR was the last to fly with tip tanks. Seen at Shannon during 1975, she awaited a cargo of livestock bound for Venice. While her operation in Europe was brief, it did not go unnoticed. Her every move was watched with great interest by enthusiasts and airport authorities alike

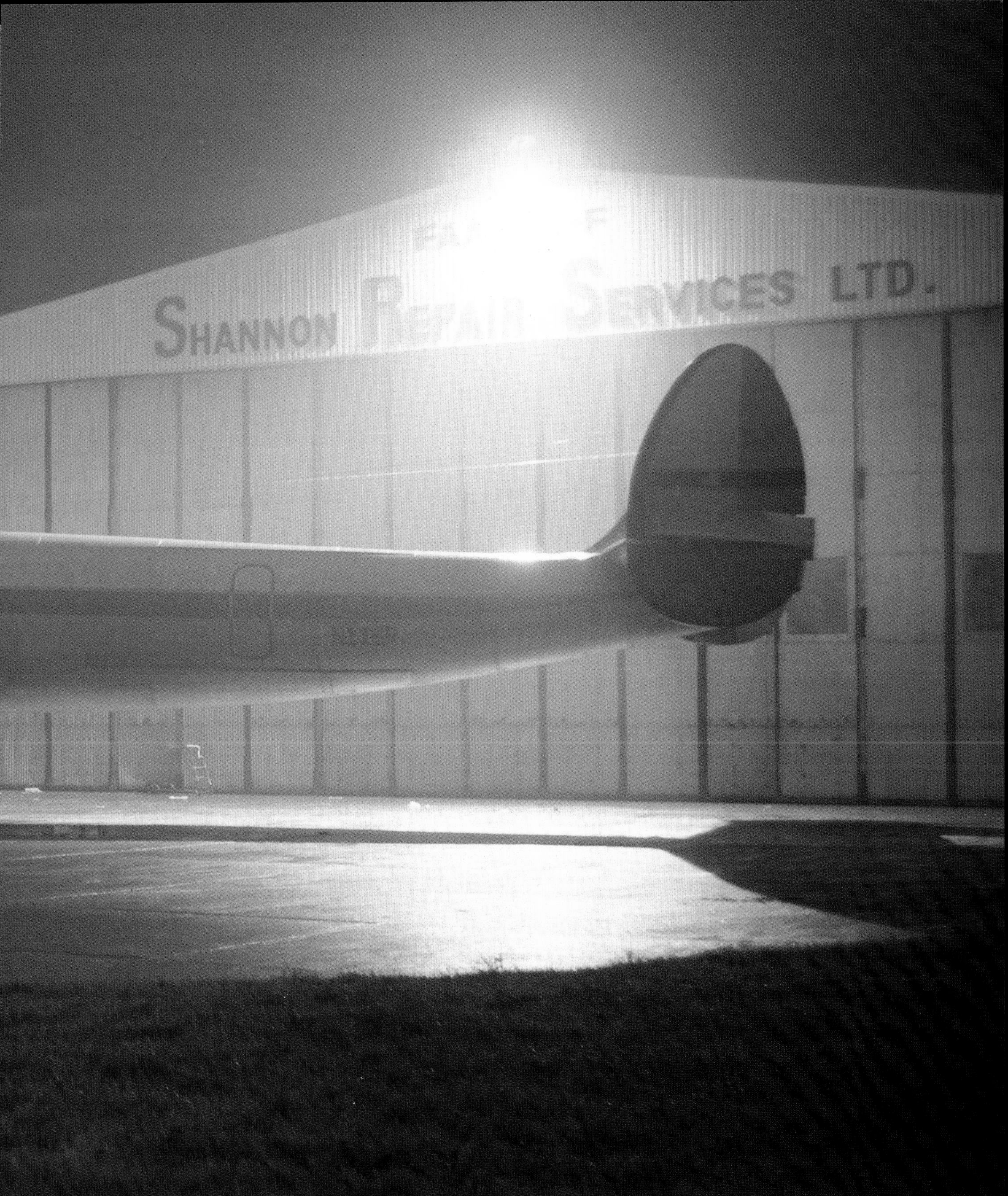
SHANNON
SERVICES LTD.

To supplement its fleet of C-46s Transportes Aereos Bolivar imported this former military C-118/DC-6A CP-1338 into Bolivia in 1977. Her career was shortlived, for in May 1978 she failed to get airborne from Inglaterra Airstrip in Beni, Bolivia, and crashed in a lagoon claiming three lives

This old DC-7C hauled cargoes of fish, avocados, mangoes and fishing tackle to points in the Caribbean during the late 1970s. In more recent years she was grounded by the FAA with a staggering 120 airworthiness violations. A record? Probably not

OVERLEAF Nose riding high, Curtiss Commando *Junia* continues to fly with Servicios Aereos Bolivianos despite a number of serious crashes (and subsequent rebuilds) in which aircrew have been killed. Some say that her construction plate is probably the only original part. Photographed at La Paz in November 1977

Workhorse of the Caribbean for five years was the Air
Cargo Support Super Constellation N1007C. Seen
uplifting produce at La Romana in the Dominican
Republic, she was retired from service and flown to
Opa Locka Airport for storage in February 1982

Although LANICA no longer exists, its successor
Aeronica is still believed to fly this C-46, AN-BRG, on
domestic passenger services within Nicaragua. This
beautiful relic was seen at Puerto Cabezas on the
eastern coast of Nicaragua during a fuel stop. The same
aeroplane OVERLEAF visited Waspam on its weekly 'tour'
around the country, the airfield being home to a large
herd of cattle. Here she boarded a group of English
Jehova's Witnesses

While Colombian maintenance occasionally leaves a lot to be desired, its brightly painted liveries beat them all. Lineas Aereas La Urraca flew an all-red, blue and green Dakota in the late 1970s, HK-1315 arriving at Bogota on a cargo flight in February 1977

RIGHT With the unlikely name of Sunjet, this DC-6B served points in the West Indies for many years. Regular ports of call were St Kitts, San Juan and the Turks & Caicos Islands

BOTTOM Old BOAC DC-7C still going strong is N9000T of Seagreen Air Transport. Registered in Antigua, but officially based in Miami, '9000T was taking on a 36,000 lb cargo of eggs for a midday 'egg-run' down to Kingston, Jamaica

'boats and amphibians

1974 was the last year that Ansett Flying Boat Services flew its two Short Sandringhams between Sydney and Lord Howe Island in the Pacific Ocean. Sold to Antilles Air Boats for proposed operation in the Caribbean, the unique flying boats are sorely missed by the Australians

LEFT An idyllic Caribbean sunset watched from a Short Sandringham of Antilles Air Boats over the Virgin Islands in 1976

OVERLEAF A peaceful setting for Sandringham VP-LVE on an Irish lake at 5 am. Later that day, heavily laden with fuel, the old flying boat took to the air for a transatlantic crossing to Gander

Take an $80 ride from Miami on a Chalk's Grumman Mallard amphibian and spend a lazy day exploring Bimini in the Bahamas . . .

. . . or travel to the Virgin Islands where you may also island hop in a Mallard. Services once offered by Antilles Air Boats are flown by the Virgin Islands Seaplane Shuttle

Faced with the difficult task of updating its old flying boat fleet, Chalk's now flies a fleet of 28-seat Grumman G-111 Albatross conversions. The boats link downtown Miami with various islands in the Bahamas

OVERLEAF The St Croix, US Virgin Islands seaplane base was always a hive of activity in the days of Antilles Air Boats. Two Goose and a Mallard are serviced for early afternoon departures to St Thomas, San Juan and St John

Venezuelan Corporacion Ferrominera Orinoco (Orinoco Mining Company) used two Catalinas to ferry crews to and from a dredger that worked the Orinoco River 365 days a year. YV-O-CFO-4 was photographed with the dredger in piranha-infested waters off the small town of Barrancas. She sank in shallow water shortly after when an undercarriage door remained open during a water landing. Two Canadair CL-215s replaced the ageing, but immaculate Catalinas in 1979

Palm tree-fringed beaches would be a more suitable setting for this Sandringham than the unnatural surroundings of Boston Harbour. This was the occasion of the flying boat's return to the Caribbean after an epic visit to Europe in 1976

RIGHT A non-flyer since 1958, this Short Solent, one of two in existence, is being restored by a small team of flying boat buffs in San Francisco

Incredible hulks

LEFT Miami's last Constellation has been unglamorously daubed *Clipper Dick* by airport firemen. This 1049H Super Connie N1880 (last flight 1977) will be burnt

'We'll get her outta here before the first snowfall' claimed 38-year old Maurice Roundy. In November 1983, after seven inactive years, his gracious 1649 Starliner N7316C flew away from Stewart Airport, New York. Her arrival at Auburn-Lewiston ABOVE was filmed by local television crews

OVERLEAF Guatemala's Aviateca flies a fleet of DC-3s on domestic services. TG-ATA was a casualty in 1978 when she crashed into a swamp near Flores

An unscheduled cartwheel landing at Frobisher Bay in
Canada's North West Territories resulted in substantial
damage to this Kenting Dakota, CF-OOY. Nobody was
injured, but the Dakota was left in the deep snow

When landing at San Juan's Isla Verde Airport in
March 1978 Carolina Aircraft's DC-6 N6103C suffered
left main gear failure. She swung off the runway and
ended up nose-first in a nearby ditch. Deemed
uneconomical to repair, she was stripped of parts and
scrapped

BELOW A propeller broke loose from this F & B
Livestock Super Constellation over the Gulf of
Honduras in 1976. Slicing into No 2 engine, it severed
vital hydraulic lines, resulting in a forced landing at
Belize with two wheels lowered. Barely damaged,
N468C never flew again. Today her fuselage is the
most talked about chicken-coop in Belize

World's last flyable 049 Connie, N90816, is parked at Fort Lauderdale. She hasn't been in the air since arriving from California one stormy day in 1978. Basically airworthy, the Connie is going for a song

LEFT Last of the three Sikorsky VS-44s, N41881 sat inactive at St Thomas for many years after a brief career with Antilles Air Boats in 1968/1969. In poor condition, this prized relic is now undergoing restoration for static display in a Connecticut museum

Weathered, but still as good a looker as the day
she rolled off the Burbank production line. Air Cargo
Support's Super Connie N1007C was later given a
cheap coat of paint to hide her age so that she could
appear in a television commercial for the Goodyear
Tire Company

LEFT Non-cargo Douglas DC-6s have a pretty bleak
outlook. Without cargo doors or floors they are
practically worthless. Nobody wanted N90749. She was
torn apart in Florida

RIGHT Once a specialized flower transporter, Aerocosta
became tied up in the drug world and ceased operating
in the mid 1970s. Its fleet of DC-6s lay scattered in
Colombia and Florida

A small number of surplus military Boeing C-97s have arrived on the civil scene in America. Powered by massive Pratt & Whitney R-4360 engines of 3500 hp, this example may occasionally be found in Alaska hauling oil or fish. She was auctioned in Arizona during 1980 as 'lot 64', hence the number hastily sprayed on her nose

American dream? Running two years late, California's Classic Air still hopes to carry sightseers in its former US Air Force and Navy Super Constellations to the Grand Canyon and other tourist sites. While the FAA appears to be having apoplexy over the idea of passengers riding in old Constellations, it looks as though Classic Air will soon be airborne. One aircraft (N1104W, in the foreground) already has seats installed, taken from an El Al Boeing 747

OVERLEAF Constellation 749 OB-R-833 *Santa Rosa de Lima*, one-time flagship of Rutas Internacionales Peruanas (RIPSA), lay derelict in a military compound at Lima in 1977 with three similar aircraft, a ten year accumulation of dust and grime being the least of her problems

During a sandstorm one memorable night in 1976 Lanzair's Super Constellation N11SR *Janet* arrived in Kuwait. With heavy construction equipment, and no cargo manifest, she was impounded without further question. There she lay untouched for six years, complete with a crate of unopened Coca Cola bottles and copies of her last flight plans scattered on the cockpit floor – just as she had been abandoned by her embarrassed crew. Auctioned in May 1982, the Connie ended up as scrap. Rumours that whisky had been smuggled into the country in her wing tip-tanks are unfounded

Constellation N273R entered service with Lanzair at a time when its Super Constellation was 'out of commission' somewhere in Europe. Her life with this adventuresome company ended in Togo, West Africa, where she arrived on, shall we say, less than 50 per cent power. Months later the old 749 was destroyed by fire in suspicious circumstances

OVERLEAF Typically Bolivian: Peasants' washing hangs out at *El Alto* Airport in La Paz, strung across the cargo area. A pair of Transportes Aereos Bolivar C-46s undergo some form of maintenance outside the airline's corporate headquarters

CP-576 was one of two rare Consolidated C-87 Liberators that transported meat and oil across the Bolivian mountains until as late as 1972. '576 remained stored at La Paz crammed full of spare parts. She was eventually traded to the USA for display in a USAF museum in California

The infamous Panama graveyard, home of just about
every South American living creature, also boasted a
DC-6, Constellation, Lodestar, six-and-a-half C-46s
and half a Douglas B-23 Dragon during a visit in 1977.
The former Western Airlines 749 and Aerofletes
Internacionales C-46 are seen in this view

Something completely different

LEFT In 1978 a group of Dominicans demonstrated how an aircraft should not be transported. The fuselage of a grounded Dominicana Carvair had been torn apart (they called it dismantled), and was being shunted by crane on to a low loader for transportation into the city. The helpless Carvair received considerable damage

Relocated alongside the Hotel Embajador in Santo Domingo, the Carvair is set among retired buses and except for its bulbous nose, is barely recognizable. Outer wing sections stick vertically out of the ground, and her four engine cowlings have been mounted on the top of the fuselage. By 1983 the aeroplane had still not opened as a cafeteria

LEFT Section of Constellation 749 engine cowling points customers in the direction of the novel 'Super G' bar and restaurant in the Portuguese Algarve. Adjacent to Faro Airport, the 1049G last flew in the Biafran Airlift. Derelict for many years, she now stands beautifully restored in landscaped surroundings that feature a pool and a drinking terrace on the top of her starboard wing

Old 049 Connie N864H started her non-flying career as the Crash Landing discotheque in a northern suburb of New Orleans. Renamed the Village Place, she offered 'live entertainment, dancing and libations'! Wearing a gawdy maroon colour scheme, the Connie was pulled from her concrete plinths in 1983 and dismantled. Business for the old bird was not good

RIGHT Old cargo planes usually lack the most basic comforts. But not this Curtiss Commando. Her crew insisted on the best

Last hauling cargo for Spanish charter carrier Trans Europa, this DC-4 became known as the Bar D-3 in Porto Cristo, Balearic Islands. She was destroyed in 1983 when a madman set himself alight